I0696037
This book belongs to:

Golden sunshine, warm and bright,
A meadow's beauty in the light,
Dancing flowers, colors bold,
Nature's wonders to behold.

Meadow Magic
A Summer Flowers Coloring Journey
with Enchanting Poems

Welcome to "Meadow Magic: A Summer Flowers Coloring Journey with Enchanting Poems," a delightful exploration of summer's most enchanting meadow flowers through the art of coloring and the beauty of poetry. This captivating book invites you to experience the magic of nature's flora as you immerse yourself in the vibrant colors and poetic verses that celebrate the wonder of summer meadows.

With 24 hand-drawn illustrations of intricate and delicate meadow flowers, you'll find your creativity blossoming as you bring each image to life. Paired with each illustration is a heartwarming and inspiring poem that captures the essence of these beautiful flowers and their enchanting surroundings.

Whether you're a coloring enthusiast, a poetry lover, or simply in need of a relaxing and inspiring activity, this book is perfect for anyone who appreciates the beauty of nature and the transformative power of art and verse.

Revel in the serenity of summer meadows, and let your creativity bloom as you journey through this magical collection of illustrations and poems. It's time to unlock the Meadow Magic within you!

Whispering breeze through petals sway,
Meadow flowers in sweet display,
A symphony of life and grace,
In this peaceful, verdant place.

Daisies white and buttercups gold,
A canvas of beauty to unfold,
Gentle hum of buzzing bees,
Nature's symphony upon the breeze.

Lavender whispers, sunflower dreams,
Meadow life is more than it seems,
Tiny creatures, secrets kept,
In this haven where they've slept.

Sunlit meadow, a floral array,
Where the heart is light and gay,
Fields of color, love and cheer,
Summer's beauty draws us near.

A sea of blossoms, colors bright,
Dancing freely in the sunlight,
Endless hues and fragrant air,
A meadow's beauty beyond compare.

Petals soft and stems so green,
A world of wonder yet unseen,
In this meadow, life abounds,
Nature's bounty knows no bounds.

Wildflowers stretching toward the sky,
A floral quilt of colors lie,
In this meadow, time stands still,
Beauty in nature's perfect thrill.

Butterflies flutter, meadow sweet,
A summer's day, a joyful treat,
Nature's brushstrokes on display,
In this meadow where we play.

Meadow's song, a gentle hum,
Nature's beauty, simply sung,
A harmony of life and bloom,
In this field, our spirits swoon.

Summer meadow, flowers fair,
A tranquil place to rest and stare,
The world of beauty all around,
In this haven, peace is found.

Gentle meadow, nature's womb,
A sanctuary in full bloom,
Life and love in colors bright,
A summer's day, pure delight.

Hidden treasures in the grass,
A meadow's secret, time will pass,
Life and love, a dance of grace,
A gentle touch on nature's face.

In the meadow, colors shine,
A tapestry of life divine,
A world of beauty to explore,
Nature's gifts forevermore.

Meadow flowers, colors bold,
Nature's story to be told,
Petals soft and leaves so green,
A summer's day, a lovely scene.

In the meadow, life's embrace,
A symphony of love and grace,
Nature's wonder, colors bright,
A summer's day, a true delight.

Blossoms sway in warm embrace,
Meadow's beauty, gentle grace,
Life's sweet nectar, colors bright,
In this haven of sunlight.

Wild and free, a meadow's charm,
Nature's beauty, never harm,
A world of wonder to be found,
In this haven of sweet surround.

Meadow flowers, a dance of hue,
A summer's day, a world anew,
Nature's palette, colors bright,
In this meadow of pure delight.

Summer meadow, vibrant, alive,
Nature's beauty, where dreams arrive,
A canvas painted with love and care,
In this meadow, joy is everywhere.

Gentle meadow, life abounds,
Nature's beauty knows no bounds,
In this haven, love resides,
A world of wonder to be prized.

Sun-kissed meadow, colors bright,
Nature's beauty in plain sight,
A symphony of life and grace,
In this meadow's warm embrace.

Flowers bloom, a meadow's cheer,
A summer's day, the joy we hear,
Nature's tapestry, colors blend,
In this meadow, love transcends.

A meadow's dance, a soft ballet,
Nature's beauty on display,
Petals sway in gentle breeze,
Summer's magic, nature's ease.

Fields of color, wild and free,
A meadow's song, sweet harmony,
Nature's beauty, full of grace,
In this summer meadow space.

Farewell

As our journey through the meadow comes to an end, We hope you've found joy in each curve and bend, With every flower and poem, a moment to treasure, These meadow memories, you'll keep forever.

May your heart be filled with warmth and delight, As you recall the meadow's beauty so bright, And as you close this book and go on your way, Carry the magic of summer meadows each day.

Thank you for joining us on this enchanting stroll, Where nature's wonders and poetry console, We hope this book has brought you cheer, And that you'll visit the meadow again, year after year.

Get more Poem Coloring Books at:
www.pencil-playground.com

www.ingramcontent.com/pod-product-compliance
Lightning Source LLC
Chambersburg PA
CBHW081539250726
48659CB00009B/3012